T0064680

TEARS, TORTURE,

— *and* —

Tomorrow

ASHLIE WEEKS, ESQ.

ARCHWAY
PUBLISHING

Archway Publishing books may be ordered
through booksellers or by contacting:

Archway Publishing
1663 Liberty Drive
Bloomington, IN 47403
www.archwaypublishing.com
1 (888) 242-5904

Because of the dynamic nature of the Internet, any web addresses or
links contained in this book may have changed since publication and
may no longer be valid. The views expressed in this work are solely those
of the author and do not necessarily reflect the views of the publisher,
and the publisher hereby disclaims any responsibility for them.

Any people depicted in stock imagery provided by Getty Images are
models, and such images are being used for illustrative purposes only.
Certain stock imagery © Getty Images.

ISBN: 978-1-4808-5987-6 (sc)
ISBN: 978-1-4808-5988-3 (e)

Library of Congress Control Number: 2018902523

Print information available on the last page.

Archway Publishing rev. date: 2/28/2018

*To all my animals and my friends who never
judge and always love unconditionally.*

Foreword

by
Ebony McCauley

WAIT! This isn't your typical foreword so please don't flip the page, pass the table of contents and get to the "good stuff!" I'll try to keep it brief, but want to give you a bit of insight from a bestie point of view of the author's work you are about to read.

I'm proud to call Ashlie a friend and often times a sister. We met over 13 years ago in Atlanta via a mutual friend and saw something in each other that had us fast becoming friends. As with most journeys through adulthood, you sometimes pull back and lose touch, maybe even get caught up in life and not talk much to a friend. One thing is for certain, that when it is true, no matter the time or distance, true friends remain friends for life.

I say this because Ashlie and I have been through a lot together as friends, and sometimes, we walk the road "alone" but realize it's not something we can or should do. Some of these poems speak to a time when Ashlie walked that walk alone. Not letting anyone know the situations or suffering others put her through. Sometimes you need that alone time to really search who you are, and with words like what you are about to read, the time and meditation helps trigger something inside you that says "I can continue on..."

Ashlie loves to help others in need, whether it's during good times or the rough road, she wants to help. So I hope you feel that support as you read these poems through your tears and laughter.

Introduction

I thought so long about how to introduce my first collection of poems. It seemed as if that process was more time consuming and laborious than drafting the prose, and even today, I feel as though my introduction is quite inadequate, but here I am and away we go.

I first hope that my words resonate with people—that they feel moved by what they read and that at some level, we connect, either through shared experiences, empathy, or simple understanding. I have traveled many roads in my young life and I am excited to see what lies ahead of me. For so many years I feared the next morning and condemned the day. During that time I felt incredibly lost and I struggled, wondering what on earth my place is here in this world. I would sit down, whenever I felt compelled, to draft a poem about what was going on in my mind at that exact moment, whenever I was struck by an idea, whether I was in the car, at dinner with friends, laying in bed at night or at work in between projects. In theory, I was recollecting a situation, or was outright quoting someone, but it was always, without fail, a feeling in the moment that I needed to transcribe.

You will find some of these poems quite powerful and perhaps a bit "messed up." And by "messed up" I mean disbelief that someone who is supposed to love you can actually say and do such things to you. They can and you must not let that break you. I bear no cross more burdensome than anyone else and I have zero requests for pity. I simply want to share my own experiences to perhaps help someone who may have gone through the same things I have been through, or perhaps are today still going through those same things and are merely trying to make it through each day, just as I found myself doing, time and time again, and unfortunately, sometimes hour by hour or minute by minute.

Other poems in this collection may make you laugh. It was absolutely my intention to intertwine some entertainment in with the serious recollections and observations. It's a very hard thing finding levity in some distinct subject matter, but for each person, there is a method of survival and at some level, we each have to respect that. Every person perseveres, survives and moves on in their own way and in their own time and dictating to someone exactly how that should be done is not always the most effective means of support.

I have also addressed some thought-provoking and quite timely issues such as gender discrimination, sexual harassment and sexual assault. Having experienced my fair share of this ugly historical "right of passage" (which seems to be the unfortunate case for so many women), I needed to set a speaker to my voice and try and reach as many people as possible who also deal with this, have dealt with it or in a very sad way are terrified of it looking ahead. This is a very despicable aspect of the life of a woman and we ALL must fight the good fight to eradicate it in every way possible.

The rest of these poems are thoughts on love and relationships in general and how we do not always know what our future holds and that is absolutely ok. For so long I fought so hard against that notion. A type-A personality, driven, together, and somewhat "standardized" in her approach to life, but when I finally stepped aside from that tight grasp that did me no favors, I was able to dream again and believe that concepts and theories and certainly hope can materialize one day. It can become tangible and you can see it and not just believe in it. For so many of us, that is the hitch. We have to see it to believe it. We have to touch it and it in some weird way must acknowledge us in return for us to understand its truth.

When you assimilate grief, sadness, fear, turmoil, misunderstanding, doubt, envy, loneliness, agony, and defeat, you are left with what appears to be the end of the world. You may find yourself staring at walls not just complacently, but inadvertently and time slowly becomes your biggest enemy. These feelings can alter who you are for the absolute worst. Take the time to get the help you need and reach out to those who love you.

Harness those emotions for the better and make them the stones of your integrity foundation. It is hard, and sometimes seems impossible, but create steps out of objects people throw at you, not insurmountable obstacles.

Contents

That First Night.. 1

In the Bathtub I Wept 2

Don't Be a Pussy 3

You're No Supermodel 4

Whore 5

You Were Unaware 6

Your Education Is Worthless... 7

I Hate It... 8

I Woke Up Today.. 9

Shut the Fuck Up 10

When You Think of Me 11

It's No Mystery 12

Hitting Leaves Evidence.. 13

It's Been a Long Time.. 14

What To Do 16

Daylight 17

I Saw A New Side.. 18

Today I Found A Hero 20

It's Ok Not To "Supposed To" 21

Be A Good Man or Walk Away 22

Love Didn't Lose My Address....................................... 23

Cool Breeze at My Back.. 24

How Do You 25

Rose Petals of the Soul... 26

Where Are All the Good Men.. 27

I Still Talk to You Everyday 28

I Can't Be Saddled with Getting to Know You 29

Get Over Yourself 30

On The Backs of Women 31

Slow Dance in the Rain 32

It Has Been My Honor, My Friend 33

When She Speaks Out 34

Her Voice Now Echoes 35

She is You 36

I've Wrestled with the Devil 37

In the Heat of the Second 38

This Woman Stands Firm 39

When Your Fear Slips Away 40

You Are Loved, Good Men 41

Finding Love on An App 42

You See What You Want 43

When She Collides 44

Friendship 45

Why Do You Hate Me 46

Missing You 47

Please Be A Leader 48

Bully 49

She May Dance Alone Now 50

Just Believe 51

Thank You 52

That First Night

I looked at you, wanting a good man;
four hours later, I knew my life was a sham.
Alone in the room, on the bench by door,
curled up in a ball, a love no more.
As you sat in the lobby with everyone but me,
the beautiful day I could no longer see.
Alone on the bed and lost for the night,
waiting for you was like a long, drawn-out fight.
Several hours passed, and you arrived in the suite:
separate showers and few words, we did not meet.
Clearly your "love" had self-serving measures,
and once I perceived those, I began guarding my treasures.
The words I spoke that day meant *our* life,
while the lies you read meant degradation and strife.
The kiss was empty and foreign to touch,
and you circled around such meaningless stuff.
Back in the room, I watch you as you sleep.
I cry, my heart breaks, and our promise won't keep.
I wake in the morning—alone—and dressed,
waiting to leave this mistake of a mess.
A trip, a vacation, a lifelong dream—
what possibly takes my mind off these things?
Talking, kissing and possible lovemaking,
but that falls short as you have been faking.
But not what you think, what you may even hope,
but promising a dream that long ago broke.
We return home, and the switch is flipped.
I am the back on which you walk and the heart that you ripped.

In the Bathtub I Wept

Each and every night before I went to bed,
I filled the tub and recalled things you said...
"No one likes you, and I choose you last;
your fears and pain are not in the past."
In the bathtub I wept again,
just as before as it always had been.
The day was long and sad for me;
no water, no salt would set me free.
Your utter contempt, your face, your look,
your hatred, your disgust were the pages of my book.
In the bathtub I wept once more,
my life, my work, they were such a chore.
Living alone, crying at night,
dreaming of peace and things made right.
The day would end and I would try to see
the morning, the week and what was left of me.
What you deserve—what should happen to you—
is beyond my control; but it's no longer true.
In the bathtub I wept for the very last time.
Without you not near me, it's my time to shine.

Don't Be a Pussy

The pool looks nice against the setting sun;
so pleasant, so peaceful it could be such fun.
We sat and talked on the porch that night,
unusual for us not to be in a fight.
The calm was short-lived as our eyes soon met.
I asked for your help, which I would regret.
Put a lock on the gate so I feel safe at night;
being alone here so often, it would be right.
"If someone will rape you and kill you at will,
no lock, no protection will stop them still."
"Don't be a pussy," you continue with me,
and then walk away and leave me be.
I breathe so deeply, and my head falls low.
I close my eyes and wish I could go
far away from you, from such shocking pain.
But I sit there, a pussy, with only my life to gain.

You're No Supermodel

What are you doing, showering in the middle of the day?
What's going on you never did say.
My picture, posing, for a designer in town:
she loves my look in her beautiful gown.
Do you get paid for this, or is it all free?
No, she's a friend; its just something I'll be.
"You're no supermodel," echoes down the hall.
You are right, it's true, I belong in a stall.
In the mirror I glance, completely alone,
ashamed, and scared, without a home.
It's terrible these feelings you instilled in me.
It wasn't just looks; it was all I could be.
Drenched in sorrow, in the bathroom I cried.
I dressed and finished and sat down and sighed.
I turned away from the reflection right there;
it was so hard to move, so hard to care.
I had nothing to say as I left the room,
you sitting there in what had become my tomb.
Later that night, alone again,
my picture so pretty but not within.

Whore

So much fun, going dancing at night—
my favorite thing; it feels so right.
I look so pretty in my dancing dress,
my hair so full, just a thick mess.
At my favorite bar, with music so loud,
we join your people, a dancing crowd.
With your best friend and you right beside,
I dance away, dance away, with nothing to hide.
"Whore," you shout as you walk away,
leaving me there with nothing to say.
I follow you quickly to find out what's wrong:
the walk to the car, it felt so long.
"How could you dance with him and not me?"
"He's your friend; we're all dancing, what could this be?"
I did not touch him, dancing afar,
but you call me this name and dash to the car.
In front of these people you embarrass me again;
it's as if you intend to, like it's always been.
I should have left you there and walked right out,
but I tried to see what could make you shout
such a horrible name that I don't deserve.
Your timing, your hatred, had no reserve.
The mirror to your face is why you call me this name;
after this, after that night, it was never the same.

You Were Unaware

My head hurts to bad, my stomach so sore;
every day, all day, it's just as before.
For one whole year, my body just breaks.
I can't keep moving, but I have to fake
my way through each day as you couldn't care less.
I bleed all the time; I am a clear mess.
Her snout in my stomach again each day,
she tells me it's wrong in her own special way.
I mention I'm sick, and I think it's a tumor.
You disappear that day, just like a brief rumor.
Alone I head to the doctor that day,
scared and sad, just to pray.
For three days and nights, I wait and wait,
wondering alone, *what is my fate?*
You were "working late" and nowhere around.
I was crying and worrying but finally found
a loving kiss, a warm embrace;
it's a cold nose, a fluffy face.
I will not die, I am told that week,
I passed it on, but you hardly speak.
Once removed and then at home,
trying to recover, I was alone.
You disappeared again for the entire day,
doing God knows what; you never did say.
Doctors explained I needed some rest,
but my money was low, and what was best
was not possible with you around,
you had things to do and could not be found.
Back at work, I was testing my fate.
I could have died, but you could hardly wait.
You hoped what had not healed would simply tear,
but my body was strong, and you were unaware.

Your Education Is Worthless

Working each day with you in my life
was so very hard, so full of strife.
Trying to balance your words and deceit
against a tough world, I could not meet.
Expectations, roles, all out of reach
from you, I tried, I could not beseech.
One day in the kitchen you look at me,
"Your education is worthless, don't you see?"
Mouth agape, I stare at you;
you try to recover, but it's all through.
What else is left to take away?
You break me down each and every day.
I worked so hard to be who I am.
Shame on you, shame on me, for giving a damn.
What's worthless is what's deep inside you—
so pitiful, so pathetic, so very untrue.

I Hate It

So many things wrong with just you and me;
so hard to balance all that I see.
Losing my family, one after the other,
so much death, I tried to recover.
A loss of not one but five so dear,
four of whom you saw with me so near.
Two animals gone, so close in time,
you brushed it off, but they were mine.
Sickness and loss, so often in years,
you complained, it was hard; you added tears.
"I hate having to tell you someone is dead."
Gee, I'm sorry for you, it's all in my head.
You blamed me for the pain I felt
as if I brought on all I was dealt.
Life is so hard, but you made it worse
with your lack of shame and heartless verse.
Today I realize you made me strong;
it was *me* who beat *you* all along.
I hate it for you that you hate it for me.
I couldn't care less as I have set you free.

I Woke Up Today

I woke up today without you here;
it was amazing, it was abundant, it was so very clear.
In my bed alone that night.
Alone was good; it all felt right.
I slept at peace, sadness set aside,
by myself—*alone*—with nothing to hide.
The day ahead brought no shame.
I smiled and laughed; nothing is the same.
I weep no more, throughout the day.
My life is good I simply must say.
Looking back so far, how did I survive?
I knew no evil until you arrived.
I woke up today without you here.
It was light, it was nice, and I have no fear.
I glance around; the change is strong.
I feel alive inside, and my life is long.
Should you feel the need to check on me,
please remember that I set you free.
For years and years I was dead to you,
but I woke up today, and we are through.

Shut the Fuck Up

Lying in bed, I shook and cried,
screaming out loud; but you just sighed.
A nightmare—someone was choking me tight.
I thrashed about and moved in the night.
The room is big, but I screamed for you.
Your anger was clear so what did you do?
"Shut the fuck up," you kicked me and said,
my pain and doubt so heavy in our bed.
Still not awake, I am lost in fear,
a dog with its paws shakes me near.
She rolls me over so that I wake up
and licks my face; such a good pup.
Annoyed, you get up and stomp away.
I am left there alone with all that you say.
My leg is sore, and I try to rest,
knowing that leaving you is simply best.
Who kicks someone having a terrible nightmare?
You do; no doubt you do not care.
I did not sleep that night in our bed.
How could I with the devil not just in my head…

When You Think of Me

I moved far away please leave me alone.
Do not text, do not write and do not touch your phone.
When you think of me, know I am safe and sound.
A life, a future; it's all I have I found.
You taught me some lessons I could do without
but I was chosen for those without a doubt.
I would have taken a bullet for you any day.
Little did I know *you* held the gun my way.
When you think of me know you have no place
in my thoughts, in my time and nowhere in my space.
I am free from you and all your ugly ways
and your terrible face and all the worthless days.
I am strong and noble and tough and true.
So when you think of me think not of you.

It's No Mystery

Glancing in the mirror, she sees her smile is lost.
Staring down her age, her dreams have come at a cost.
She's been battered and beaten, abandoned and bruised,
kicked and pushed and quick to lose
her faith and hope how they hide deep within
but tomorrow is new and she begins again.
It is no mystery why she's broken in half
and it is no mystery she wants to take it all back.
He pushed into her life only wishing her pain.
He tore piece by piece and she'll never be the same.
For years and years she struggled and fought
for a whole new woman and that's what she got.
But it is hard to recall when there was a time
she knew honest men who drew the line.
Memories fade and love persists and dreams do not expire.
Back in that mirror she looks up again and now she sees the fire.
But she's ready and tough and wild and free—
through hell and back she can finally see.
The good, the bad and what comes next;
for now, forever; nothing but the best.

Hitting Leaves Evidence

As we ride in the car, I can't help but stare
outside, at everything, I do not care.
We are together that day but I'm all alone
in the morning, at night and in my broken home.
Where we were going, I seem to forget;
it never really mattered, but then ours eyes met.
"I wish you beat me instead of what you do."
"Hitting leaves evidence and then I'd be through."
Ahhhh… you, your job and your cruel family
and protecting number one is all that you see.
Your words, your actions and your heartless ways
and your hatred, your intent and all the painful days.
You broke me down and stole so much
and my dreams were lost to your cold-hearted touch.
You got such pleasure out of making me cry
each day, each night and every time you passed by.
You were such a big man having taken my will.
I stayed by your side and loved you still.
I glance back outside to see things un-changed.
How foolish I was as it was all the same.
It all hurts, always and no matter what the form;
your life, your happiness—from all that you're torn.
Away from the monster I kept turning my head.
It *all* leaves a mark no matter what you said.

It's Been a Long Time

It's been a long time since something went right.
She tries and works and continues to fight.
Daunting, hard and simply unfair
each day, each week so why does she care?
What hope is there when failure is near?
No job, no family—nothing but fear.
To express in words what empty is like
always falls short with no end in sight.
The mirror acts as a painful reminder
that trouble and agony are not far behind her.
Abuse, death, sickness and loss
has been her life at such a high cost.
It's been a long time since she smiled so wide
but the weight of failure cripples her sides.
She buckles and breaks and falls to her knees
begging for peace from anyone, please.
With all the travesties, virtually one each day
she has no time to brush the pain away.
It's been a long time standing on her own.
She trips, she stumbles, she has nowhere to go.
Life continues its daily battles for more
but at this point she has been in a long drawn-out war.
Battle-weary after ten long years
but it simply fails to produce any more tears.
It's been a long time since she actively dreamed
as if her soul gave up and all that could mean.
For so many years she cried and cried;
will he hurt me, will he lie or will he force me outside?
At one point she seemed to run out of tears.
It's been a long time, crying every year.
It's as if the mistakes are on repeat
but nothing has happened to yet unseat
this dread, this loneliness and innate despair

but she desperately searches the will to care.
Where does she go to believe in her worth?
She tries a big, risky and new rebirth.
It's been a long time since her arrival in state,
but she pushes and pushes and is told to wait.
The bricks that sit on her very small frame;
the weight on her shoulders—it's always the same.
It's just another day that tracked her down
and tested her limits, cracking all around.
What does make her bend is not the past
despite what those doctors told her last.
The burden of failure drops her to the floor
because nothing is working here anymore.
Where does she find the strength to proceed?
In her mind, in her heart; her soul must lead.
She digs deeper in, farther than before;
a tickle of faith—is she pushed for more?
This corner she backed into so long ago
in irony always there and all that she knows.
Battle-weary, broken and lost inside;
the war ongoing—it's a bumpy ride.
Yet still she must rise above all on her own
and life will continue to battle it's shown.
It's been a long time and years have gone by
alone on that field and she just has to try.
Shields up, heart smart, and intellect brace you.
Bring on the battle because you're never through.
"Things happen for a reason," she's told each day,
so she'll push and fold in her own special way.

What To Do

It's supposed to wash all the bad away
and the day begins again.
But sitting alone inside my room
the rain is not my friend.
I thought one day I would run out
of tears and loss would subside.
I look around my empty house
and all I can do is hide.
So much I've lost and persevered and tried to look ahead.
But frankly now, sadly now, I simply wish I was dead.
Who would care and who would grieve
and who would wish it not so?
Many I'm sure, who could never move on
but right now I just don't know.
What lies ahead when hope is lost
and you haven't dreamed in years?
What would I look like asleep at night
without such pain and fear?
I would not guess or begin to know
what that could ever be.
I try to picture a life of peace but it seems impossible to see.
I push ahead like I always do because that's what's expected of me.
For now, right now, to continue the fight
it's all that I can be.

Daylight

The sun is out and it's clearly daylight
but the darkness still rolls in.
Today this life, this time for me
is exactly where I have been.
I don't understand how nothing could change
despite all that I have done.
Each day is the same and on repeat
and sluggishly in place I run.
The battles that form a life of war
never at all subside.
You push and choose what truce to call
and set the rest aside.
When you love and do what's right
and move from deep within,
the hatred that lives in other hearts cannot possibly win.
If you find darkness falls heavily all around
just look for the light on the battlefield
and that's where victory is found.

I Saw A New Side

I saw a new side of you today
and my heart simply broke, I have to say.
I had opened up to you and your difficult ways
knowing how limited empathy is these days.
But you are someone I have known my entire life
who has watched me every day weather agony and strife.
People I loved were killed or died
and alone in my room I sat and cried.
A lost career and abuse I fought every day
and for years and years from my friends I pulled away.
I only had you as an outlet from fear
but you mocked me and broke me, and then brought it near.
Animals taken during this time too
but you said it was stupid; there was nothing to do.
Deathly sickness on and off through the years
and the pain and agony brought so many tears.
"Oh poor Ashlie, oh poor you;
you're weak, it's in the past, and you fail at what you do."
I can assure you this encouraged me not one bit
and today I saw you don't give a rip.
For ten seconds you became a stranger to me
and he was standing right there and he's all I could see.

I have struggled to pursue the reason to be
but now, with your words, I can finally see.
With failure comes loss and loss becomes pain
and your feelings are personal and it's your heart to gain.
Work on yourself when no one is watching,
careful to see who you are.
Stay true to your life and beliefs and core, and you will go very far.
Drown them out those who don't empathize
and dig deep inside and avoid all the lies.
Harness your pain and flip it around
so those who doubt have no voice to be found.
Make them see what they did and how they had a choice.
Some will wish they could take it back and provide a loving voice.
The rest don't care, and certainly don't love
and sadly will continue the fight.
It's empty against strong, but you push and grow
and that's what makes you right.
For we cannot banish those we love to an
island for something they said.
So if you love and need them look around and try not to be misled.

Today I Found A Hero

Today I found a hero.
A hero I discovered is me.
No longer ashamed and scared
and a bright future is all I see.
Surviving so much death and illness
and tragedies and obstacles and more.
Each night as I would lay down,
for peace and warmth I would implore.
Grit and failure work together
and create a woman so strong.
The rocks thrown at me from all sides
built the path I've walked all along.
Those who questioned and doubted me
weighed heavy on my mind.
But at the end of a very long struggle,
encouragement in them I would find.
The sun shown down on this woman
with beauty and humor and heart.
I was striving to uncover the rest:
sheer will and force from the start.
Today I found a hero
believing I can conquer at will.
For tomorrow I am finally ready
and my beliefs will be with me still.

It's Ok Not To
"Supposed To"

So much advice from everyone—
from loved ones and those you don't know.
How do you arrange your feelings?
So many directions in which you can go.
It's hard to juggle so many things
as life can be so unreal.
Your partner, your job, your health and faith;
so many things in which you can feel.
What happens when all this falls at your feet
and everything is going wrong?
All these choices you face at once
and each day drags on for so long.
You're "supposed to" get out and be seen
and you're "supposed to" be in the sun.
You're "supposed to" mingle with friends
and you're "supposed to" go out and have fun.
While all these suggestions are right
and you may or may not want them to be,
for it is ok not to "supposed to"
because you know best what you need.
Sometimes when life bangs at your door
you can answer or pretend you're not home.
It's ok to simply step away
because it may be best to be alone.
Perhaps "supposed to" works when there
but sometimes it's not right for you.
Take heed of what your heart says
and to your core you must be true.

Be A Good Man
or Walk Away

Be a good man or just walk away.
It seems so simple but yet you stay.
You mock me, you laugh and you tear me down.
All in an effort to build your own crown.
Be a good man and treat me well;
encourage and support—I should not have to tell.
Do not pretend to be someone you are not;
whether in words or form or whatever you got.
So many guys run around each day
taking advantage of all in their way.
Be a good man and above them stand tall;
it's such a nice surprise seeing them fall.
We stand here together debating this day
and you can't help but try and take my smile away.
Why do you do this— to make you seem strong?
Has your scheme so far been fake all along?
Make good decisions and choose what is right
and be a good man and join the good fight.
If you cannot have the heart of a good man,
just walk away because you can.

Love Didn't Lose
My Address

For so many years I wished on countless stars
and watched as couples held hands from afar.
Does it hurt the most to have loved and lost
or never have seen love—what is that cost?
Caught somewhere in the middle I would be
until I met you and I could finally see.
Love lost my address for so long I thought
but all these days waiting were very well fought.
So far away I glanced at you
and you raised your head up and what did you do?
You stared at me and smiled with your eyes
and my knees went weak but my grin was a disguise.
I didn't pretend I wasn't taken by it all
and despite the large crowd you were all that I saw.
Finally before me you begin to speak
and at that point it wasn't just my knees that were weak.
I saw that I moved you in the exact same way;
a reaction on both sides new to me I must say.
Hours later there was no doubt in time:
me for you, and you are mine.

Cool Breeze at My Back

I see you and your bold brown eyes and handsome face.
I feel you here and you invade my space.
Welcoming this man so new to me
but here you are, no place I would rather be.
I was surprised when you moved toward me that day
and it was the first time a man took my breath away.
We talked and laughed and you smiled at me
perhaps in a way to set us free.
So many people watching so close,
you and I the same, guarding what means most.
I looked up to you to read those eyes
and at first you resisted but then it passed by.
The mountains behind us, a cool breeze around
and your warm touch at my back, perhaps I have found
someone like me and just as strong
because I'm ride or die and we ride all life long.
We part briefly to speak to people there
and I politely listen, but I just don't care.
Across the room our eyes meet once more
and you smile that smile and motion toward the door.
See and be seen at the party that day
but not many saw us because we slipped away.
The cool breeze over the mountains by the shore
and any doubts I may have linger no more.

How Do You

How do you make it through the day
and honestly where is your brain?
For anyone else around this place
it would be boring and each day the same.
I am staring at you simply in shock
and processing your idiocy.
But I truly can't because I know what should and should not be.
You seem to try as your eyes glaze over
but your effort simply won't do.
The biggest feat in your simple life
is successfully finding your room.
What did I do to deserve this fate
standing here today?
You continue with making my head hurt
and I wish I was far away.
It's like trying to have a full conversation
with a pillow on your bed.
And then wondering aloud, "I better turn down the music
because I can't hear what my pillow just said."
How do you make it through the day
and not get hog-tied to a tree?
I guess your purpose in this life
is to balance our own insanity.

Rose Petals of the Soul

Sometimes I'm a blazing fire burning bright in the evening sky.
Sometimes I'm a trifling candle glowing softly soon to die.
Sometimes I'm a raging river fiercely flowing into the night.
Sometimes I'm a tiny creek trickling its way out of sight.
Sometimes I'm a brave lioness, fearless with strength as her core.
Sometimes I'm a baby kitten hesitant about wanting more.
Sometimes I'm a solid boulder—an obstacle blocking the course.
Sometimes I'm a little pebble weak and unnoticed from a source.
Sometimes I'm a bellied laugh enjoyed and felt from the heart.
Sometimes I'm a very slight chuckle quickly
dismissed from the start.
Sometimes I'm a tragic tear ripping its path down a face.
Sometimes I'm a weary sniffle held back by time and place.
Sometimes I'm a forgotten thought empty as a blanketed hole.
Always I'm a human being—capable of emotions from the soul.

Where Are All the Good Men

A very strong woman knows what makes her so unique.
She pursues what she wants and typically
finds what she dares to seek.
Some things are elusive and she can't help but wonder why
she finds herself among these men just to simply pass by.
She consoles and commiserates with friends who get it too
and they talk and laugh and make it light
because what else can one do?
"Where are all the good men," she asks, "I
think they're in earth's core."
You first need a Sanskrit map and a magic shovel—what a chore!
Find a leprechaun to guide you and a unicorn to ride
and wait for the stars to align and an eclipse to find.
Find a dozen four leaf clovers and perform a ritual dance
and wait for Moses to part the waters
again, and then take the chance.
"Where are all the good men?" she asks and no one can reply.
It's just a waiting game for her and alone she sits and sighs.

I Still Talk to You Everyday

You will killed 15 years ago on that dreadful night.
I screamed and cried and was really quite a sight.
You were my uncle, my friend and my father in ways
and I still talk to you each and every day.
Your smile and laugh always so dear
and alone I sit without you here.
I miss you and wish I could be so close
and our time in town is what I miss most.
You did not judge and only embraced
and the look you gave was always true face.
When you left us so quickly I could have just died.
It was so hard to hear that and I just cried and cried.
At your service, your casket so real—
anger and resentment was all I could feel.
So young and loving and the best man I knew;
my disbelief just grew and grew.
For so many years I rejected your death
because without you here, I could not accept
the thought that I could never hug you again
or talk on the phone as it had always been.
And now so long after leaving us here,
I dream of the day you are again so near.

I Can't Be Saddled with Getting to Know You

You seemed so nice as we texted and talked,
even speaking of spots where we could ride horses and walk.
Your grandmother so ill but you at her side
was such a nice thing to be close to and by.
For days we spoke about our lives and dreams;
meeting the right one which is so hard it seems.
You pursued our first date like a personal mission
but little did I know facts were all fiction.
Our first date would be dinner at a place close by
and you would pick me up and together we would drive.
You asked if you could drink and let loose for a while—
of course I said; that doesn't get me riled.
The next day you requested a spot in my room
but I had not met you and this was far too soon.
I hesitantly told you my guest room was there
but I thought how strange just don't get impaired.
The next morning a text arrives in my phone
and it was incredible that message and what was shown.
"I am looking for a relationship but now just sex
and if that's not ok, let's cancel what's next…
I can't _suffer_ through conversation and all that mess
just to sleep in your guest room," (it was too much I guess).
Are you even human—do you have a heart?
Where in your life did you get this start?
How horrible for you that you live in this way
but thank God I found out with no "suffering" that day.

Get Over Yourself

I'm not here for your amusement
and I'm not listening to the lies.
I work hard at this job
and I keep my eyes on the prize.
You hired me for my face and my "beautiful" ass
not paying attention to all of my class.
I would listen to your comments about looks and frame
and each day I sat cringing at the sound of your name.
I was just out of school and you were seventy-one and
"gramps," I thought when my interview was done.
Some days would pass without you near
and I would thank my stars to be quietly clear.
Offering to buy me what my heart desired—
clothes or trips; what would not get me fired?
"I would like to take a bite out of your ass and get lockjaw,"
you said to a young woman one day in the hall.
Out of your office after a meeting one day
you come from behind and grabbed me some way.
Your hands on my shoulders and you near me
and you kissed my neck and hatred I could see.
I resigned the next day as quickly as I could,
making a choice to move on if I should.
Years later you murdered your wife in your home
but the law was slow to make that crime your own.
You died soon after before your time
and your offense was finally brought out to shine.
What a horrible person you were from the start
trying to own people while from honor you part.
Sex and power was all that you knew
but now burning in Hell is what you magnificently do.

On The Backs of Women

On the backs of women so many men have stood
rising in ranks and doing all they could.
To build their lives on deceit and pain,
and destroying these ladies again and again.
In positions of power they rose to the top.
Never looking back, just damaging non-stop.
It was of no consequence how they made their rank
and the company ships; they simply just sank.
No one knew why this never worked out
until now all these women begin to shout.
"We matter too," they say so strong
and you cannot do this as you have done for so long.
On the backs of women you have made your disgrace
but now we have voices and we are in your face.
We are no less than you and shine just as bright
but for so long your shadows were blocking our light.
Today no longer do we hide in the weeds
and tomorrow is ours and it's our field you need.

Slow Dance in the Rain

Slow dance in the rain with me please this night;
you are so handsome in the dark moonlight.
Your arms are so strong and your heart is so good
and the night is warm and I know that you could.
The evening was lovely with you at my side
and we stepped out from dinner and under the awning we hide.
But the rain falls down around us so near
and I love to have you close with me here.
It's a busy night with folks all around,
but in this place I have finally found
a man who makes me laugh and sing and smile.
I have been looking for you for such a long while.
"Slow dance in the rain with me," I quietly ask
and in true love I can finally bask.
The umbrella drops from your hand just now
and you take me to the street among the busy crowd.
In the middle of the road you hold me close
and the rain pours down and we make the most
of that moment "alone" in the sweet summer air
and they watch us—each one—and we do not care.
For no one else in the world exists but us
and we dance in the rain with no reason to rush.

It Has Been My Honor, My Friend

It has been my honor, my friend, to know you so long
and see you develop into someone so strong.
For years we have been a part of each other,
as friends, we are sisters, just from another mother.
When you hurt I hurt, and I wish I could heal
whatever it is that makes you feel
like giving up and going away
because life is so hard for us some days.
But the struggle, the loss, the agony and the pain
makes us who we are today and it's all a gain.
I share in your fear and your hope for more
and if I could I would make it what *I* bore.
I would gladly lay my life on the line
to protect you and let that bright light of yours shine.
Each day we have forged a friendship so close,
despite the miles that make it the most
difficult to maintain what we hold so dear
but our commitment is to each other and I am always near.
I pray you find that special man
who loves you and wants you and does all he can.
For you will always have me to lean upon
no matter what life throws at us and no matter when it's gone.

When She Speaks Out

When she used to speak out heads looked the other way.
Her words and her actions were a glimpse in the day.
She moved against a tide so fierce
and her heart would break each time it was pierced.
She was forced to hide and retreat in shame
but now she can bluff this all-male game.
Minutes were years and the days passed by
and she could only be left to question why.
To hear these women speak out in turn
allowing each lady to redeem what she earned.
It's bringing to light what was shadowed till then;
it was women and the public; not just all men.
When she speaks now heads turn *toward* her
and listen so close as her words clearly stir.
She's captured the world which was so insane,
without you, who cares, she's driving this train.
She is charging forward in all that is right:
the past, the present and always leading the fight.
Stand with her in this crowd so deep
and find your bearings and simply draw on her speech.

Her Voice Now Echoes

Her voice now echoes down the halls where we are
and you see her now, no longer from afar.
She is in your office and your home and your school
and she no longer allows you to play her the fool.
Her words are strong and ring loud in your mind
and her depth and worth are for ALL to find.
She's been silently screaming and sobbing for years
but a solid front has hidden her tears.
No longer will she sit quietly in the dark
and wonder who next will make their mark.
Now you can sit and listen and meet
this woman whose voice now echoes in the street.

She is You

She is you, my friend, my partner, my boss.
She's waited so long and she has been at a loss.
She is in front of you, behind you and always stands near.
Her strength and courage are not to be feared.
She is smart and capable and honest and true
and she's the backbone of life and all that we do.
She's a smile, a tear, and a move the right way
and she is our future, our hope and armor in the fray.
Watch her and follow her and revel in might
and pick this woman to join in the fight.
For she is all of us in this world so lost
and respect and equality come at a great cost.

I've Wrestled with the Devil

I've wrestled with the devil so God must exist.
For as long as I can remember I've tried to resist.
For one without the other does not reason make
and for my future in whole I cannot forsake.
It's difficult to believe when you cannot see
and if not impossible when it is all so ugly.
Year after year you struggle and fail
and watch as your life is beyond the pale.
He or she hates you, they wish you such ill;
every minute you fight and it's all uphill.
At home, work, or out during the day;
you are up against the devil in every way.
Fighting and watching and waiting for light
and every minute is hard but He knows what's right.
You doubt and linger over all that you've become
and sometimes it's hard just not to succumb.
Dark needs light and light will persist
and that devil will rise no matter how you resist.
Know that all things occur as they are meant to be
and latch on to your faith which sets you free.

In the Heat of the Second

Every moment you are near me, my body is on fire
and if I denied this intensity, I would be a liar.
Your hands, your embrace and large blue eyes
keep me listening and watching long after you pass by.
In the heat of the second I fell for you;
your passion, your depth and all that you do.
It wasn't just how handsome you are
but your smile and laugh I noticed from afar.
There's something in my gut that dances around
each time you are near and it's love that I've found.
At first the sensation was so new to me,
and I doubted the presence of what it could be.
It's been a long time since I backed away
from the doubt over everything each man would say.
But you changed my thoughts and made me see
that my dreams are out there and in front of me.
Now that I have you and I hold you so tight,
I can thank my past each and every night.
For without those years and the fights I won,
I wouldn't be me and we wouldn't be one.

This Woman Stands Firm

This woman stands firm alone or with you.
She fights what's wrong and against the bad we do.
She's determined with those who say she's to blame
for her skirt or her blouse; it's all just a game.
And the question why this is just now brought to light?
Because so long ago she would have lost that fight.
Since you can't control yourself it's not her fault
but this woman stands firm because that's what she's taught.
Get it together and do what's right
and stop pointing your fingers at her in spite.
Honor should not be so hard to find
and a woman only wants some peace of mind.
This seems like such a very simple request
and yet she's engaged in this battle and endless contest.
Who has more resolve and who has more to lose?
It's this woman right here and recognition she'll choose.
If she cannot stand firm then we all descend
it's not just one person—we all must transcend.
Each day brings opportunity to share in success
and this woman stands firm to show us what's best.

When Your Fear Slips Away

Sometimes when you love there's nothing to grasp
and all of your dreams become the past.
He hates you so and wishes you dead;
such harsh words that you always dread.
How can he feel so strongly toward you?
What made him this way and what did you do?
You question how it all began
and how he breaks you with everything but his hands.
You see your reflection or catch your own eyes
and how easily someone who hates passes by.
To feel invisible is heart-wrenching and sad
but you persevere because you have had
the power to know what is and is not
and he has himself and that's all he's got.
He cannot control you and he cannot see you fall
and you are better than him and better than it all.
It's lonely and painful and it just never ends
and you ebb and flow along with the wind.
It may take some time to find yourself
with your heart in pieces up on the shelf.
When your fear slips away and you stand so strong,
you will see you won that war all along.

You Are Loved, Good Men

For all that we say and all that you read,
from the words of your friends to the current news feed.
There are such good men out there so brave and real
and we must care about them and how they feel.
We love you good men, not just for what you do
but for who you are and because you are true.
You don't play games and you don't treat us wrong
and desperately want to make up for all that's gone on.
You are loved, good men, by these bright lovely women
and we are grateful to you for all that you have given.
When women stand up and speak their minds
in it no animosity for you will you find.
You make us laugh which is our favorite thing,
and being with you, we're a queen to your king.
You are loved, good men, when you take us in your arms
and we are enveloped by true love and all your charms.
Stand up with us and encourage those around
and your strong voice is needed to stand our ground.
Be faithful to this cause and and to the promises you make.
For we love you, good men, and the bad we forsake.

Finding Love on An App

Finding love on an app and stapling butter to a tree:
exactly how effective can each of these be?
Time consuming, yes, but shocking even more
for you find so many folks whose moral fabric has torn.
Some of us seek to meet our new friends
but after one or two talks, the "conversation" quickly ends.
For some it works out and they find the one
and for others it's akin to fishing on the sun.
Its difficult to dig through the mountainous weeds
and find a decent man who is dressed above the knees.
Why on earth do I want to "naked cuddle"
after only knowing you through texts in this dating bubble?
Unsolicited you send graphic pictures of your junk,
demonstrating the ship of gentility long ago sunk.
I did not request to see your lower parts
and it would have been nice to have dinner and that be our start.
When did dating became such a silly conquest?
Don't we always want for us the very best?
Finding love on an app makes you want to give up
but then what happens if the right one is stuck?
Somewhere among the nonsense and the mindless games
he waits for you just the same.
I guess we find love where love finds us
but be sure who you swipe and be sure who you trust.

You See What You Want

I am not difficult and I am not a "bitch."
I am not some "girl" who "pitches a fit."
You see what you want and label me for convenience
but inside you fail because it's all the wrong reasons.
I've been punished for standing up for my own peace of mind
while other men walk on me to get to their own side.
If my words and actions have such deliberate force
for some reason for me you plot a new course.
One that involves being cast aside
and hiding behind my "difficult" side.
But he is late all the time and cannot be reached—
yet here I am always in my own seat.
I'm responsive and accurate and protect what's right
while he plays golf and his mindless trivia at night.
And here I am sitting in this office can
while he's untouchable because he's a man.
Unequal standards drive your thoughts
and I cannot compete with a brain in a box.
You see what you see which means you've got to go.
We cannot have men like you running this show.
Your desperation and insecurity are palpable in this place
and your inhumanity and lies have no room in this space.

When She Collides

She stands among friends or she stands alone;
her light reflects around and her power is shown.
When she collides with faith, hope and dreams
what you see before you IS what it seems.
She's brought us back to what is right
and shows us now the worthwhile fight.
She dances a somewhat dangerous dance
but she will not accept fate left to chance.
Watch and learn and understand
that all men and women should rise again.
For all what we see is not always fair
and we each must take time to truly care.
Today, tomorrow and yesterday are here
and if we risk our future there's so much to fear.
When she collides with you in concept and time
remember all these forces are best when aligned.

Friendship

We lean on her when times are dark
and so often we think it seems so stark.
She listens and talks or just nods her head
and ponders each and every word you've said.
It's that pensive look and warm embrace
and her thoughtful side and beautiful face.
She takes the time from her busy day
to trace what went wrong and got away.
She will cry or sing or celebrate with you
but give you space if you need that too.
She will dance when you dance or just sit still;
whatever you need; it's what you both feel.
She watches closely as men come and go
and some treatment she sees makes her hate the show.
For she can't make him finally appear, at last,
but she can prop you up against the pain of your past.
After all this is gone or when you're alone,
you will know true friendship after all she's shown.

Why Do You Hate Me

Why do you hate me and break me down?
Your insecurity and fear create a horrible sound.
I work just as hard or even harder than you
yet you hate me for all the things I do.
I'm smart and interesting and very proud.
You are too; I'm not your personal cloud.
What makes my success so hard to take in
when you've thrived so long despite any sin.
Side by side together we could be so strong
but you've pushed me away for so very long.
What if I was "he" instead of "she?"
Would you hate me as much or just let me be?
It's hard to know why you cuss and fight
because we're on the same side which is all kinds of right.
What if I continued to keep my mouth shut
and dwell in this deep, dark and ugly rut?
Would that be ok if I silently kept still?
Does that ease your mind and all that you feel?
What if she's your boss now or some fateful day?
Are you just mad/n enough to simply walk away?
Keep in mind we share our human insides
but not these you show now; that's your own divide.

Missing You

I miss everything about you but one special thing
has played in my mind and it's quite interesting.
Do you recall that day that I fell down and cried?
You had not seen me break and and my actions belied
that woman of steel you watched for so long
and she could not take it and her will was gone.
Instantly you sank to my side that day
and pulled me close as if to say,
"I know you and this will soon pass on
but let me hold you till this day is gone."
We sat for hours in a room with no sound
and all that was there was your love all around.
You said nothing more that afternoon
and I fell asleep all too soon.
You stayed put while I was lost in dreams
with you arms asleep no doubt it seemed.
I might have been distant but I knew you were there
because you kissed my face and played with my hair.
Was that a small or enormous display?
For me it was both on that very dark day.
Despite how I felt and the pain I was in,
I would replay that day again and again.
Just to be in your arms and against your chest,
you knew what I needed better than the rest.
So thank you for being so good to me
because memories like that enrich what we see.

Please Be A Leader

My goodness please lead in these troubling times.
What are you doing and have you lost your mind?
We like you composed and one to revere
and not at the top of all that we fear.
The world is dark and troubled today
but tomorrow brings hope despite what you say.
We look to each other to succeed all around
and in you we need a strong leader to be found.
Your mind must be clear and your actions true
for you to be who we need and do all that you do.
It's no longer personal and "me, me, me."
It's all us now and we all need to see.
Don't divide these people that can be so close
and do not rally a group simply to boast.
Please be a leader and one to admire
and not the target for such ignited ire.
We wish the best for those who take on
the demanding job of being the one.
To judge does no good but it's hard to resist
when you fight so hard against what makes sense.
If you fail we all fail and no progress is made
and many strides we've taken that we don't want to fade.
There's still time to curb this enormous downfall
and just be a leader and make the right call.
It seems so simple and yet you don't
or is it worse—yet you won't?
Take the time to measure your words
and this place you control would be far less absurd.

Bully

What makes a bully is so hard to tell.
They hide behind such an insecure shell.
She may be bold or super chic
and he may be cool and the "top pick."
Who are these people so easily found?
They move within a vulnerable crowd.
So many victims in which to choose
but we all get hurt and we all then lose.
It's the young, the small or people "they've" been
or the unique ones that just don't fit in.
A bully is lost even though they are near
it's a result of years of wading in fear.
We cannot rid ourselves of this mess
but we can take charge and teach the rest.
A bully sees no age nor sign of pain
because power is all they seek to gain.
Their forms vary greatly and come and go
within our lives but we can never know.
Be strong and stand up to all that is right
and don't engage such a silly and empty fight.
For we win when each one is held to their own
and they reap the fail and all the've sewn.
When we are not bothered and they are left to guess
these bullies are stuck in their own drawn-out mess.

She May Dance Alone Now

Looking around as the music plays loud
she sees the couples among the dance floor crowd.
She smiles with her friends despite being alone
and she will want to dance on down the road.
She has thought long and hard and come so far
and to dance tonight would just be too hard.
It takes time to piece it together and heal
and push aside the pain that she feels.
That night she'll dance alone in her room
for to be in his arms is simply too soon.
Deep down inside the clouds can part
and she's absolutely ready for that amazing fresh start.
Sometimes she must just step aside
to push away that doubt in her that hides.
Some part of that will always be there
but her heart of gold she can't help but share.
For she danced alone so long in the storm
that dancing alone now must not be the norm.
It's different today to have that control
for not long ago the steps took their toll.
He will ask again and she will agree
to that dance of hope and then she's free.

Just Believe

We each have a life we are here to live
and that life alone is ours to give.
We can do wrong or we can do right
or we can walk away or engage the fight.
We can choose to make the best of what's here
and always protect what we hold dear.
Just believe in yourself and what you can share
because that's all that matters as you are aware.
Time can be an obstacle and a blocking force
but you push around and stay the course.
They will attack and try to overtly dissuade
but you cannot let go of all that you've saved.
Just believe in the mirror and what sits inside
and from the darkest of corners you will not have to hide.
It will be hard and trying on you,
but time is us and we make it through.
It may seem like the choices are all so poor
but life is funny that way with what's in store.
Each move we make defines our next act
and against any evil we must never crack.
Just believe in the power of true honesty
and you need not second guess your own dynasty.

Thank You

Thank you to all those who encouraged me here.
Your thoughts and wishes I will always hold dear.
We each must find our way in this place
and sometimes we fail and feel a disgrace.
But failure is learning and learning is success
and I can do that alone but with you is best.
Today I have put a pen to my mind
and what's unknown I'm excited to find.
Sharing what's in our deepest of hearts
can make you feel small without the right start.
And the love that is there when you speak to me
truly is all that I ever will need.
Thank you for never mocking my thoughts
and for being a shoulder when I was distraught.
I can't tell you how much you bring to each day
for the good, for the bad—each trial we weigh.
I never heard you call me a name
and your intentions for me were always the same.
To find happiness and be free of fear
and you did your part being so very near.
I was never weak in your thoughtful eyes
and this alone was such a welcome surprise.
Thank you for never judging me
and offering your love unconditionally.
Today a woman evolved from so much,
but it seemed less harsh with your gentle touch.

Printed in the United States
By Bookmasters